THE MUSICIAN

poems by

Robert Simon

Finishing Line Press
Georgetown, Kentucky

THE MUSICIAN

Copyright © 2017 by Robert Simon
ISBN 978-1-63534-320-5 First Edition
All rights reserved under International and Pan-American Copyright Conventions.
No part of this book may be reproduced in any manner whatsoever without written permission from the publisher, except in the case of brief quotations embodied in critical articles and reviews.

ACKNOWLEDGMENTS

The Department of Foreign Languages and the College of Humanities and Social Sciences for their support of my work in the allowance of time and a generous subsidy;

The Atlanta Freedom Bands, for having given me a space in which to return to music;

Finishing Line Press, for your faith in my poetic endeavors;

Friends and family who have always been there; and

To Helena and Sophia, my lovely muses.

Publisher: Leah Maines

Editor: Christen Kincaid

Cover Art: Robert Simon

Author Photo: Robert Simon

Cover Design: Elizabeth Maines McCleavy

Printed in the USA on acid-free paper.
Order online: www.finishinglinepress.com
also available on amazon.com

Author inquiries and mail orders:
Finishing Line Press
P. O. Box 1626
Georgetown, Kentucky 40324
U. S. A.

Table of Contents

Three Voices 1

The Proposal 3

Twenty-three Minutes 4

"You can't play the clarinet anymore" 6

As Estrelas 8

Absolute Zero 10

The Wine 11

Hautbois 12

66th Birthday Call 13

O Beijo e o Voo 14

Editing 15

The Good Christian 16

The Flower 17

Toasting the Decade 19

To an unjust Rejection 21

A Notícia duma Possível Vergonha 22

A word on love 23

Leave Taking 24

Three Voices:

Wind from among Sabbath trees
A cold, abrasive reed aloft
Impressive moorings on the lips and
Keys from double-sided major chords

An orchestra of tongues,
Moonlight sonatas in three apical points,
A cold, abrasive reed descends
In each, a section from a tune,
Germanic or Romance or brass perhaps,

So unlimited in scope, yet
Already at music's end,
A saxophone plays English vowels
Stepping with each note before the other
Yet without an end to its vocabulary,
A diction unfulfilled;

In short work the tongue moved on,
Such a clarinet sounds, deep vowels
Push forth quickened turns of small,
Agile cars in the streets of Madrid,
So very lost in the multiplications,

Until the song came to be,
Seemingly from reeds floating in dance,
Along the banks of the river
Visible from the open roads of the Bairro Alto,
One above, one below, in harmonious
Vibration, singing Mozart or Scheherazade
an oboe calls in her double tones.

This orchestra of three bodies and four tongues,
A moon beyond three points of light
In early hours, the wracked reed and warm breath,
They'll melt droplets of sun and dew,
A romance set for the music of polyglots.

15/XII/2015-27/I/2016

The proposal:

WE walk again here, you and I,
Like scraps upon grandfather's table,

A delightful sampling of phrases
From sources old and new, rehashed,

Semantics of soup, and a dash of commas,
And just for fun a semi-colon, or two,

We place again our feet forward, one by one,
In tearful gesticulations, an errand of fools,

Contributions of flies, a soup indeed,
Heaped upon the bowls in such a dire array,

This hamper full of lexical laundry, clean
Until the dawn, the soiled again by type,

Until he's used them all up, sipped into
An ancient, indecent tongue, then stepped

Beyond the delights of graves, old sources
Made new as we stroll by black-slick shores.

18/VII/2016

Twenty three Minutes:

Walking, running,
Chatting about useless topics
Like car accidents or your not knowing
The difference between a comment on Facebook
And a peer-reviewed article in *Hispania*.

Walking, running,
Chatting about twenty three minutes
And how I couldn't look you in the eye
After you looked at the ground
As though it owed you something.

Lapping the grasshoppers again
Chatting about your favorite technique
My aunt must have heard of in college,
The birds come down to feast
In the morning frost and you spout on about peer-reviewed
Facebook posts, or should I call it your edited opus.

Then today, two weeks later,
You wouldn't look me in the eye,

Perhaps you thought you saw me on Twitter
Performing a bad book review of your
Latest Instagram exhibition.

Walking, running, chatting
About your shoes or how good
The warm weather felt last August
Perhaps you thought we could hear you
Above the din of the mower crossing
The green, looking for the next accident.

Or maybe you thought I would post
This poem on Facebook and get some
Feedback and out-publish you.
Walking, running, chatting about useless topics.
Lapping the aphids this time, snug
In their adorable little holes, believing
They couldn't possibly be wrong.

3/21-4/28/2016

You can't play the clarinet anymore

When it's been sitting in its case under a desk
For two decades without a man's touch,

Only the bedbugs have shown it the proper caress,
Reeds dwindling, a canyon in the wind,

I placed her bell upon the lower joint, of course
There was almost no cork left, so I

Had to stroke some paper in between her worn ends,
The memories flowed so readily back then,

How the music had never really come to me,
Jazz or opera alike, how we sat,

She and I, upon a bench declaring how
In like we were with each other,

When she asked me to kiss her, and I did
Because I knew better even then,

The scent of mold and uncared keys sits
Now, braced in the push from a space heater

In a basement full of all sorts of loving
Embraces, hidden in file folders

Or the saxophone case under that same
Desk my grandmother used to own.

She passed on in 1993 of dehydration
And never finished that family history;

Yet I digress, words flowing back from
The neck with her golden ring so worn down

It pains pictures' sensibilities, cold to the touch,
Two decades and I just had to put her away.

16 February 2016; 21 March 2016

As Estrelas:

Vi uma estrela
Que luzia na noite

Como se olhasse para mim
No espírito afoite

E disse-me, grandioso,
Que o jogo começou

Quando os dias nasceram
E o sol a levou

...

Naquela noite compus
Um poema de mais baixa
Qualidade, repleta de ritmos
Vadios e rimas rentes,
De aliterações de alicate
Numa meia-noite de chuva como o chumbo entre penas,

Naquela noite vi uma estrela tão alta
A luzir no meu cortiço vertical
Entre lábios tensos e línguas soltas.

Vi-te, e alcancei-te com a voz da noite.

Vi-te, e amarrei-me com a tua voz de luz.

...

Uma estrela, bússola em cores,

Uma lua, mãe acidental de todas as luzes

20-23/VI/2016

Absolute Zero:

They appeared on the 15th
After a smile and bright eyes
That love me,

No one else has seen them,
Not even when the camera
Caught me,

Yet the five-eighths dance
Heard them, singing out
Upon me,

In Eastern modes transmuted
By Reed and keys in motion
That saw me,

Open both left and right,
Air pressured to move forward
Into the crowd,

No one else has seen them,
Not even with the seats
So closing in,

Arpeggios collapsing forward
From heavenly moods and
Choral traps,

Toward absolute zero in
Armenian Dances and
Wrinkled eyes,

Then clapping rings out,
And we're happy when
It ends late.

24 / IV / 2016

The Wine:

And I sat to watch
The lone tree with no straight
Branches in a parking lot slowly
Waving good-bye in the November
Breeze,

      The young man in the *Perú*
t-shirt staring at nothing for
long as he finished his lunch
glasses off,

      the doll in mommy's four
year old arms not moving
at all, receiving butterfly
kisses,

      and a deep misty wind
      blowing leaves away

This arpeggio of yellow and brown

19-20 / XI / 2011, Kennesaw, GA

Hautbois

Alone, quiet
In soft darkness
You sit in the hope
I will place my hands
Around you in
Aromas of saliva and wood

Taken from blackness
Into the air, held lovely
And with such finesse

Together, cutting
Through silence
You and I make the world
Tremble in our wake.

Tomorrow, perhaps, or today
As paper planes in a low breeze
Or a happy runner in the morning dew

19 / VII / 2016

66th Birthday Call:

It was good to talk with you this afternoon
After the political debate on Facebook
And the belief that you mean only the best

Even when supporting a plagiarist,
And I'm so glad you had a good day
After so many when you thought you were

Going blind, and as a reminder you
Forgot to put your glasses on and realized
Only as soon as you tripped over the sheets

On the way out of your low bed, it was
Really good to talk with you and think
About when we could catch up without

A political debate or why your granddaughter
Should visit or why I just can't tell you these
Things anymore

19 / VII / 2016

O Beijo e o Voo:

As escovas escorregaram na tua direcção

Sentimos um estremecimento entre nós,

Cheguei a crer na tua boca, deixa-me saber
Se as asas da borboleta te tocaram alguma vez

Nas bochechas, naquele museu em Houston

Sentimos um estremecimento entre nós,

E as escovas escorregaram na minha direcção

Cheguei a ler que o voo não aterrou
E que a borboleta nunca mais te pôde tocar

Os pés escorregaram para baixo, para mim,

As asas chiaram com o zumbido duma nuvem
Térrea, verde como o limo ou o novilho,

Sentimos um estremecimento entre todos nós.

29/VI/2016

Editing:

Did you think they wouldn't notice
When you vanished and never called back?

Did someone set ablaze your rationale
Or did you hand them a match and turn around?

Did you think you could simply vanish
As a sliver of carrot from the dinner plate?

Did someone hand you a pass
And wish you the best of luck out the back?

Did the rain finally wash you away
Without a moment's hesitation or even your number?

The Good Christian:

You sit with me,
White shirt at day's end
Talking about the weather
And calling him a Jew
(while the little girl dances)
(while the music plays)

As a rambling rhinoceros
Would at the worst of all
Tea times, conscious only
Of the Klimt or Pollock
Before him,

Or a professor with no
Doubt as to green-blue
Seas in triplicate,
Its split envelope such
A lucid reddened fearing
Heathen song at daybreak

You sit with me, beliefs intact,
A motor rolling over a vehicle
Or a manger burnt to a green ash.

(While the girl dances)
(While the music plays)

9/VI/2012
Acworth, GA

The Flower:

From Lublin he came,
having flown over Dresden
and Paris and Places who
made his country less German
more Russian and several
bags of peanuts and filtered
water in pretzels later he
took the escalator up to the
baggage claim and didn't
know why those people were
applauding

Then he learned how to
rent an apartment and get
a job serving tables and earned
a living smiling and
doing what he had done for
her, the one he left on a
swing in the park that almost
sunny afternoon when
he saw the glint of
early summer and unborn
children playing through her
gaze

before hours of seeing nothing
but open ocean beneath him, cut
only with the Azores and JFK,
he took

a napkin and in seconds made
for my daughter a white rose,
and took his tip and thanked us.
Obrigado, dziekuje, e bom trabalho,
seu Marco, ¹

24/XI/2011
Kennesaw, GA

---

[1]English:
Thank you (in Portuguese), thank you (in Polish), and good job, Mr. Marco,

Toasting the Decade:

12 April / April 12th:

Shifts in the direction a leaf fell today

Reminders of how little exercise I've had lately

Streams of breeze between branches

In two days I'll be forty
And no one would have known the wiser

Steps down the grey hallway carpeted in mashed paperclips

Shifts in sheets of old essays to shred

Reminders of how little we've exercised today
Or how a dying father's last wishes are so far from my static hand

Streams between branches, breath of northerly dreams.

13 April / April 13th:

In forty two minutes my thirties end
What's left to say about that
Except to give my warmest thanks
and send my best.

14 April / April 14th:

No more leaves ran away, as did I,
Since this morning's meandering, five miles long,

Oranges blossomed somewhere cognisant
And I bellowed out a joyous song of songs

No more reminders will stand firm
And trains may now resume their steady clip

Today the world has learned
The words of calm demeanor from my lips.

12-14 April, 2016

For the occasion of my 40th birthday

To an unjust Rejection:

Perhaps we should begin again

At the cherry tree, or maybe

At the shrub, or even, quiçá,

At the level of dirt, yes, light brown
Dirt drenched in remnants of feet
Filling its spaces with portions of
The bottoms of chinelos born from
Dead wire from the 70s, when they
Fought here,

Or perhaps we should sit down
Over um bom café com leite
And decide if you had the right
To say those things, out of place
And now out of sight,

Down where the brush meets the road,
Where the beetles find their lunch
Or where nove angolares compram o almoço
Da multidão, those heaving piles
You ignore to tell me I do not know
How to cite sources,

Yes, let's begin at the level of dirt,
A reddened boot perhaps, sandy remains
Of hope,

At the shrub, my cherry tree, where
I'll begin again.

15 / VII / 2016

A Notícia duma Possível Vergonha:

Impactantes são as palavras
Como "voo cancelado" ou "chegámos",

E quando recebi a tua mensagem
Hoje à noite e lá fora caíam os primeiros
Flocos de neve, oh, meu amigo,
Quantas palavras sentia por ti e por eles,

Um cordão de guitarra, cinco dedos
Ou a nasalidade do concerto em dó,

Uma palavra, duas, ou três
Que são os dedos de passeios e sem voz,

Os segundos passavam lentamente,
Cães aflitos pelo clima frígido e sem abraços,

Impactantes são, as palavras
Como quando nós chegámos, embora eles não.

8 / II / 2016

A word on love:

A word
                on

Child goes
Through the woods,
Child goes
Through the door,
Child goes
Through the crass waves

              Controls to watch whatever

Comes to   mind

                              Would waves

Rush over me

        Or would their voices
As a child goes
    As waves

        Child goes

                To the deep blue sea
And she'll
    Sail with me

Through the woods

And drink another drop of ice cold love.

26/X/2011-2016

Leave Taking:

The musician continues to walk
In paths of light stone and in circles

When the sun's hampering can do
No harm, as if to say it has had

Enough of quarter notes and letters
Or in other short words

It's had enough of long steps with
No real grasp of its own strength,

And such is my sullied tongue, to you,
That in each day's mulling around

Please try not to wake the dragon
Too quickly, she has a temper

And your e-mail address and
Never did like the saxophone that much.

25 / VII / 2016

Dr. Robert Simon was born in Saint Paul, Minnesota, and is Professor of Spanish and Portuguese at Kennesaw State University. He has taught Lusophone and Hispanic languages, literatures, cultures, and literary theory, and has investigated the presence of Surrealism, Mysticism, Postmodernism, and Transnationalism in Contemporary Lusophone African and European, Peninsular Literatures, including the poetry of modern Galicia.

His current books of literary criticism include *Understanding the Portuguese Poet Joaquim Pessoa* (Edwin Mellen Press, 2008), *The Modern, the Postmodern, and the Fact of Transition* (University Press of America, 2012), and *To A Nação, with Love* (Argus-a, 2017).

In terms of original poetry, Robert Simon has published several poetic collections including *Summer Poems of You and Me* (Finishing Line Press, 2011); *Poems of a Turning Professor: A Collection of Two Epochs in Five Parts* (Allahabad, India: Cyberwit, 2015); and *Os Sophíadas* Parts I and II (Lisbon: Apenas Livros, 2009 and 2011), as well as several individual poems published in journals in the United States. His verses touch on themes of love, language, and music, attempting to reach out toward the limits and liminality of both in the 21st Century.

Dr. Simon lives with his wife and daughter in North Georgia.

www.ingramcontent.com/pod-product-compliance
Lightning Source LLC
LaVergne TN
LVHW040118080426
835507LV00041B/1760